Jonathan

Oh

Jonathan!

Lu Neil Isett

To Jim and Janie from [signature]

Published by
Time-Light Books
Van Nuys, California

To Jesus, who saved my life.

 On May 15, 1973, in an interview aired over NBC-TV Richard Bach, author of *Jonathan Livingston Seagull*, was asked if his book were, as many people believed, about Jesus. His answer was, "Yes." Then he went on to add that he was surprised when he realized that the book was, as he put it, "about Jesus, the Christ." Very probably that is correct.

The great danger of *JLS* is that as people read it, they, too, are unaware that it is about Jesus, consequently they absorb false teaching without realizing it. The only way to determine the truth of a teaching is to measure it against God's revelation of Himself. *Jonathan Oh Jonathan!* is just that, a comparison of Bach's concept of Jesus with the Jesus of the Bible.

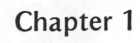

Chapter 1

One day about six
months ago I received a call from one of my
husband's brighter (and more eccentric)
students. Without preliminaries he asked,

"Have you read *Jonathan Livingston
Seagull?*"

I had never even heard of *Jonathan
Livingston Seagull*, so he said,

"I'll be at your house in fifteen
minutes."

He was.

Without explanation he laid a small
package on my coffee table and said, "Well, I
have to go. Goodbye," and strode out. I have
not seen him since.

Out of the brown paper bag came a slim,
blue volume covered with muzzy, soaring
birds. Abruptly, the Gull had landed in my
living room. And as I began to follow its
webbed tracks, I was immediately impressed

with the beauty of the book and the empty-sky freeness of it.

But before I was half finished I began to feel a real uneasiness—nothing I could put my finger on, just a little something nagging at the back of my mind. It was not too many more pages, though, before Jonathan showed his hand (foot?) and the true nature of the Gull began to emerge.

Jonathan was a gull who wanted more out of life than wheeling and screeching a few yards off the ground. He had a drive to fly that was so far out of the ordinary as to be totally unacceptable. Gulls have to conform ... it's the Law of the Flock. When Jonathan wouldn't (or couldn't) conform he became "Outcast," consigned to the lonely places always inhabited by free spirits. So far, so good. But .... Leaving earth, Jonathan was transported to a realm which he first thought to be heaven. In this dimension he learned of telepathy, the illusion of deity, reincarnation, teleportation, denial of the material world, and about a vague something called "love" which one must "work on."

It isn't all spelled out like that, of course. These ideas are casually fitted into the most charming sort of high altitude experience, carefully free from any heavy theological setting. Just an uncomplicated story of a seagull who wanted to fly, and who, because of his fearlessness in learning, became one of the transcendent ones. Just a simple gull we can all identify with. After all, isn't the book dedicated: "To the real Jonathan Seagull who lives within us all"?

When I finished the book, I was very, very sure I didn't trust Jonathan Livingston Seagull.

I began to check with others. "Have you read *Jonathan Livingston Seagull?*" I would ask doubtfully.

11

I was met with smiles and enthusiasm. "Yes. Isn't it beautiful?"

What really began to appal me was that not only had the secular world been deceived by this book, but that most Christians had been taken in, too. I very soon came to realize that the Gull was a real winner in the race for men's minds . . . and, ultimately, their souls.

In a time of focus of interest on the occult and of a proliferation of books on demon possession, Satan had really slipped one in. Everybody was looking the other way, occupied with preaching against astrology and witchcraft while, without ruffling a feather, a snowy white seagull had charmed them into helping make the devil's lie the runaway bestseller in America in 1972. Everyone was being so careful not to become possessed that they had allowed themselves to be seduced.

I Timothy 4:1 says: "But the Spirit saith expressly that in later times some shall fall away from the faith, giving heed to seducing spirits and the doctrines of demons." This comes from no less an authority than God, Himself. But though this falling away is bound to occur, God intends that His people be fully apprised of what the adversary is about so they can successfully resist him, or, as II Corinthians 2:11 puts it: " . . . that no advantage may be gained over us by Satan: for we are not ignorant of his devices."

Just as there are basic doctrines of Christianity, so, the Bible teaches, there are demonic doctrines, and they have as their source Satan, whom Jesus called "a liar and the father of lies."[1] These doctrines of demons are simple, consistent, knowable, and utterly false. Everyone should be aware of what they are in order to recognize them immediately, no matter how charmingly they are disguised, no matter where or in what form they are found.

13

Jonathan Livingston Seagull has been accepted by the majority of professing Christians for a very simple reason: it is not much different from what they are used to hearing. They are not really aware of what the adversary teaches, nor of his extreme subtlety. If Jonathan is any indicator of the sort of thing the devil will be using more and more, then the average, pew-sitting Christian is going to have to learn to recognize that which is anti-Christ, whether he finds it in print or hears it from the pulpit.

In his letter to Philippi Paul put it this way: "And this I pray, that your love may abound yet more and more in knowledge and all discernment; so that ye may approve the things that are excellent [an alternate translation is: *"distinguish the things that differ"*]; that ye may be sincere and void of offense unto the day of Christ."[2] Peter was blunter: "Be sober, be watchful: your adversary, the

14

devil, as a roaring lion, walketh about seeking whom he may devour."[3]

And if the devil can go about as a roaring lion, we should not be surprised to see him passing himself off as anything at all. The Bible says that Satan can disguise himself as an angel of light and his ministers as ministers of righteousness.[4] The Christian, then, must learn to see through the form, whether it be philosophy, theology, or fantasy, and look for the content.

Chapter 2

"Forget about faith!" Chiang said it time and again. "You didn't need faith to fly, you just needed to understand about flying."

Chiang to JLS
Part II

    Christian doctrines have a purpose. They teach the basics of the faith. Demonic doctrines have a purpose, too, and that is to destroy faith and bring chaos. This is their sole design and intent.

Richard Bach, the author, tells a very interesting story about how *Jonathan Livingston Seagull* came to be written, and he tells it with absolute frankness.[1] The book came to him from disembodied "voices," and visions. In fact, the work was left unfinished for a number of years because the first "voice" did not tell him the entire plot. Finally, after a lapse of some time, an additional vision completed the story.

19

"Voices" have to be one of three things: human speech, hallucinations, or spirit communication.

But Bach was entirely alone when the first "voice" spoke to him the title of the book. It couldn't have been a human, for no humans were around. He was alone when the plot was given to him. And hallucinations do not write bestsellers.

That leaves the problem of disembodied, non-human spirits.

The Bible deals with spirits of all kinds in a very straightforward way. "Beloved, believe not every spirit, but prove the spirits, whether they be of God: because many false prophets are gone out into the world." (I John 4:1.)

In other words, not all "voices" are reliable. One must listen very carefully to what any "voice," whether it be of man or of spirit, is saying.

John goes on to say: "Hereby know ye the Spirit of God: Every spirit that confesseth that Jesus Christ is come in the flesh is of God, and every spirit that confesseth not Jesus is not of God: and this is the spirit of the antichrist . . . ." (I John 4:2-3.)

These two verses are the key to distinguishing true Christianity and false religion. *The Number One Doctrine of Demons is the denial of the Incarnation of Jesus Christ.*

The Incarnation seems to be so basic to Christianity that there should be no confusion about whether or not anyone actually believes in it. But Satan is nothing if not subtle, and the world today abounds with groups who claim: "We believe in Jesus," then march straight into the outer darkness.

There is a great difference between "believing in Jesus," and believing that "Jesus Christ is come in the flesh," and it is necessary for us to be aware of this distinction.

21

What John is saying is that one must believe that Jesus *Christ* is come in the flesh; that is, not simply believe that there lived a man named Jesus, but that God was made flesh in the person of Jesus of Nazareth.

John fully explains what he means by "come in the flesh" in the first chapter of his gospel, verses 1-4. This is what he says:

"In the beginning was the Word, and the Word was with God, and the Word was God. The same was in the beginning with God. All things were made through him, and without him was not anything made that hath been made. In him was life; and the life was the light of men."

Here John is carefully laying the basis for his discourse on "the Word." This "Word," he tells us, was with God before the creation of the world, the "Word" was of the same nature as God, the "Word" was active in creation, and gave life to men. Obviously,

John is identifying the "Word" as the one, true, almighty, creator God.

Then in verse 14 he tells us: "And the Word became flesh and dwelt among us (and we beheld his glory, glory as of the only begotten of the Father) full of grace and truth." Be careful to understand this. "The Word," previously identified as God, *became flesh.* Jesus Christ is come in the flesh. This is a true confession.

What, then, is the difference between this doctrine and the false religions? It is this recognition of Christ as the second person of the Trinity. Many of the cults will claim that Jesus is the son of God. They believe we are all sons of God. What makes them false is this: they do not believe that Jesus is *God the Son.*

It is not good enough to believe that Jesus is one of many sons of God, or that He became God. The Bible clearly, consistently teaches that Jesus is not one of many, but that he is the *only* begotten son,[2] and that He possessed deity before the foundation of the world. Any teaching contrary to this is the spirit of the antichrist.

Besides the false teachings of universal sonship and Jesus' attaining godhood, there is the currently prevalent idea of Jesus, the Good Teacher. This humanistic approach to the Gospel permeates contemporary thinking, and, ignoring Christ's statements about His identity, focuses on the moral and ethical content of His teachings. To rank Jesus alongside Aristotle, Plato, Buddha and Mohammed is to deny His uniqueness, the Incarnation.

The late Bishop James Pike, during a seance, asked a spirit who claimed to be his son, Jim, a suicide, if he had seen Jesus. The reply was that they "talked about him only as an 'example' and not as 'savior'."[3] A woman in El Paso, Texas, who contacted a spirit through the use of a ouija board, and then progressed to automatic writing, heard the spirit speak for the first time when she questioned it about the person of Jesus Christ. "He was just a man," it screamed, "like any other man!"

Missionaries in the field have experiences with evil spirits which take possession of someone. Dick Hillis of Orient Crusades says, "We never once had a demon-possessed person acknowledge that 'Jesus Christ had come in the flesh'."[4] It would seem that demons don't like the Incarnation.

In his recent book, *Satan Is Alive and Well on Planet Earth,* Hal Lindsey reported on an interview he had with the well-known seeress, Jeane Dixon, in which she confirmed to him her belief in the following statement from her book, *The Call to Glory:* "His (Jesus') major message was if we follow His teachings and strive for the kingdom of God while on earth, then we will have a much better life on earth and the assurance of eternal life in heaven."

When Mr. Lindsey asked her why she did not explain faith and salvation in her books, her reply was, "Because the world is not ready for that yet."

This is not what God the Father thought. He thought the world was plenty ready, for Galatians 4:4-5 tells us: "but when the fullness of time came God sent forth his Son, born of a woman, born under the law, that he might redeem them that were under the law, that we might receive the adoption of sons." One cannot separate what Jesus taught from what He did.

Nor can Christ's teachings be combined with any other system of moral values into an eclectic religion. Jesus said that He (alone) was *the* Way, *the* Truth, and *the* Life, the *only* way to the Father.[5] His authority stemmed from Who He was.

Whether it is called demythologizing, Christian atheism, or called by one of the cult names, any attempt to separate Jesus Christ, God Incarnate, from what He taught is a perversion of truth.

Bach (or the "voices," as the case may be) never claims in the book that Jonathan is to be understood as a Christ-type. That idea is just "picked up" by the reader. There is Jonathan the teacher, Jonathan the healer, Jonathan the lover of the flock. You probably would never realize that toward the end of the book you are reading it as an allegory—but you are. And then he slips this one in:

"A moment later Jonathan's body wavered in the air, shimmering, and began to go transparent. 'Don't let them spread silly rumors about me or make me a god. O.K. Fletch? I'm a seagull. I like to fly, maybe . . . .' "

Jesus Christ is God the Son who stepped into human history as a man.

Jonathan Livingston Seagull is an impostor.

Denial of the Incarnation is a doctrine of demons.

Chapter 3

Most of us came along ever so slowly. We went from one world to another that was almost exactly like it . . . Do you have any idea how many lives we must have gone through before we got the idea . . . A thousand lives, Jon, ten thousand! . . . we choose our next world through what we learn in this one. Learn nothing, and the next world is the same as this one . . .

Sullivan to JLS
Part II

Nobody wants to die.
It's as simple as that. And because of intense desire not to die, the human mind almost always shuts out the possibility of death. It is just too awful to be true; therefore, it isn't true.

A very bright graduate student sat over a cup of tea with me a few weeks ago and made the following statements: "There is no heaven and no hell: when you die that is the end of it. If there were a God, He wouldn't be mean enough to punish you for not believing in Him." When I began to share with him about his two basic miscomprehensions—the nature of God and the fact that he, himself, has a spirit which is dead apart from God—his reply was, "Garbage!". And with that he got up and went home. He seemed to be quite angry.

I can only assume the reason he was angry was that he felt himself to be threatened. People who have their minds made up about the absence of God and of life after death don't want to be disturbed. It makes them insecure when the Word of God intrudes on their beliefs, because, if they ever consider that they might be wrong, not only is life in the body focused on the wrong things, but whatever life might be after the death of the body can only hold fear.

Why?

Sin.

From the very beginning there has been an identification of sin with the denial of death. Listen to this conversation which took place between a very foolish woman and someone who wanted to seduce her:

"And he said unto the woman, 'Yea, hath God said, Ye shall not eat of all the trees of the garden?'

"And the woman said unto the serpent, 'Of the fruit of the trees of the garden we may eat: but of the fruit of the tree which is in the midst of the garden, God hath said, Ye shall not eat of it, neither shall ye touch it lest ye die.'

"And the serpent said unto the woman, 'Ye shall not surely die . . . .' " (Genesis 3:1-4.)

*The Number Two Doctrine of Demons is
the denial of judgment and death.*

Sin is a dirty word. It smacks of judgment and judgment is something we humans
don't like. We want to always be thought of
as good guys, and it is offensive when
someone says: "All your righteousness is as
filthy rags."[1]

Not much is heard about absolutes these
days. Relativitism is rampant, and the situa-
tion ethic is the governing standard of the
day. Everywhere there are bumper stickers
and posters saying: IF IT FEELS GOOD, DO
IT. (It is interesting to note that there are no
signs suggesting that if it feels bad it ought
not to be done.) The critical factor seems to
be basically irrational—that is, feeling versus
logic.

When Jonathan Seagull told his students:
" . . . freedom is the very nature of his (the
gull's) being, that whatever stands against that

freedom must be set aside, be it ritual or superstition or limitation in any form," he was only voicing beliefs held by a large segment of humanity. It is conditioned relativism.

Joseph Wolpe, professor of psychiatry at Temple University School of Medicine and Eastern Pennsylvania Psychiatric Institute, says in his classic textbook on behavior modification:[2] " . . . it is justifiable to attack on rational grounds a patient's religious beliefs if they are a source of suffering." Rational grounds? Apparently Jonathan and Dr. Wolpe have been drinking from the same well.

The idea that is manifest here is this: there is no higher standard for behavior than emotion; the rightness or wrongness of a thing is judged on the scale of human feeling. It is based on the assumption that only what we feel today matters, and that nothing we do has more than transitory effect—that is, there are no eternal values.

This particular position involves two basic mistakes: a lack of comprehension of the nature of God, and no realization of what man's limitations are. The two are closely related, and result in a spiritual myopia that is disastrous.

Man is a creature living in a material body which inhabits time and space. Consequently his perceptions are limited by those dimensions. To the natural man, good is that which is pleasing for any given period of time.

God is pure spirit and is not confined to time and space. Unlike man, His existence is independent of these things, and His perceptions are not limited by them. With God time is NOW, and He sees all actions and desires as complete or consummated. He, alone, unlimited by a foreshortened view of the future, can judge the eternal value of any act.

It is because of this basic difference in natures that human desires and the ordinances of God come into conflict. We are lusting after the temporal; He is dealing in the eternal. Proverbs 14:12 tells us: "There is a way that seemeth right unto a man, but the ways thereof are the ways of death."

Sin has many forms, but basically it is only one thing: refusal to acknowledge the authority of God the Father. It is simple rebellion, very much like that of a child disobeying his parents. We know what the rules are, and we break them because we think we know more about what is good for us than our Creator does. Or, to put it another way, we want what we want more than we want what He wants. It is an unusually shortsighted point of view.

Rebellion is an affront to God. Satan rebelled and attempted to exalt himself above God, bringing terrible judgment upon himself (Isaiah 14:12-20). When a human being

39

decides that he is big enough to control his own life and scorns the authority of God he does exactly the same thing. This, then, is sin, and the Bible tells us that "If we say we have no sin, we deceive ourselves and the truth is not in us"[3] and: "The wages of sin is death . . . ."[4]

Make no mistake about this. Man chooses hell, destruction and death. This was not God's original intention for him. Hell, the place of burning, was not created for man. It was prepared for the devil and his angels.[5] If men go there, it is because they choose to go along with Satan on earth and thus become liable to the destruction God has ordained for rebellious spirits. Jude 6 tells us: "And angels that kept not their own principality, but hath left their proper habitation, he hath kept in everlasting bonds unto judgment of the great day."

Men will not willingly accept this

sentence, however, and their denial takes two forms. The first is a simple refusal to consider any existence after the death of the body.

Of all wishful thinking, this is the most wistful. It is a deliberate denial of something inherent in man . . . belief in life after death. The belief in the continuance of the spirit after the death of the body is virtually universal, and as old as death itself.

The animist in Africa has no question about an afterlife. Elaborate tombs of antiquity are mute testimonies that the people who built them believed in some sort of ongoing existence. Much of what is known about ancient civilizations comes from the grave, for those left behind were careful to furnish the departed with tools, weapons and other necessary items for his use in the next world.

Learned men of all ages have believed that the life man has in the human body is only the beginning. "Look death in the face with joyful hope," said Socrates, "and consider this a lasting truth: the righteous man has nothing to fear, neither in life, nor in death, and the gods will not forsake him."

Only rarely through history is disbelief voiced. Lucretius, a Roman poet and an Epicurean, viewed the fear of death as the source of all human ills, and finally identified this as being basically a dread of eternal punishment after death. Denying the afterlife, he set out in his works to extinguish these fears in other men and to declare the sanctity of human emotion. He died, it is generally agreed, fifty years before the birth of Christ . . . a suicide.

The denial of life after death has become more popular lately, particularly with those who consider themselves to be intellectuals, and is based on a fairly new concept of man . . . that he is essentially a machine. The basic idea (which is now very prevalent in education and psychology) is that man operates entirely on stimulus and response. The essence of this view is anti-personality, and the logical end of such a viewpoint is that when the sensory mechanisms fail to operate so that there is no more response (death), then all is over, because there was never more than that going on. That is, since man is only a machine, when the machine breaks down there is no more man. Or, as my young friend put it, "When you die, that's it."

The other form taken by the denial of judgment and the sentence of death, is an insistence that there is some provision made after death to improve one's state. In reality this is a denial of the *finality* of death, and there are millions in the world today who hold this view.

By far the largest segment of these believe that men return to life to make amends for the deeds done in former lives. Thus the ages go by in endless cycles of birth, suffering, and death. "Learn nothing," Sullivan, the gull, says, "and the next world is the same as this one . . . ."

There is not one place in Scripture to indicate that any man who has died ever returned to earth in a different human body. Not one! Surely if such a doctrine were compatible with God's revelation of Himself it would have been mentioned. Even in the case of John the Baptist, whom Jesus declared to be (spiritually) Elijah, it must be remembered that Elijah, in fact, never died, but was taken up alive into heaven. What we are dealing with here is not the return of the spirit of a dead man to a new body. It is a supernatural visitation of the spirit of a living prophet, Elijah, on one who, according to Jesus, was "more than a prophet."[6]

The Bible has a straightforward approach

to how many lives a man has. Hebrews 9:27 bluntly states: " ... it is appointed to men *once* to die, and after this cometh judgment." The beer commercial that claims: "You only go around once in this life" is absolutely right about that. Unfortunately, there is no awareness of the judgment that is waiting afterward. These two facts are inseparable: all men die once, and after death men are judged.

The Bible speaks consistently concerning this matter. Listen: "For when a few years are come, I shall go the way whence I shall not return."[7] "When a wicked man dieth his expectation shall perish, and the hope of iniquity perisheth."[8] " ... the soul that sinneth, it shall die."[9] "And it came to pass that the beggar died and he was carried away by the angels to Abraham's bosom: and the rich man also died and was buried. And in Hades he lifted up his eyes, being in torments ...."[10] "And I saw the dead, the great and the small standing before the throne: and the books were opened: and another book was opened which is the book of life: and the dead were judged out of the things which were written in the books, according to their works."[1] [1]

The people who are unwilling to believe that the end of this life signals the end of opportunity to "get right with God" feel that this finality is unfair. They think that people should be given a second chance and that it is not nice of God to deny this to them. There is never any consciousness that they have already had a second chance in this life . . . possibly an eighth or a tenth.

There is no reason to think that a soul at enmity with God would profit by endless lifetimes when it did not profit by one. Consider the witness of Revelation when time after time the judgments of God come upon the earth, and men refuse to turn from evil.

"And the rest of mankind who were not killed with these plagues repented not the works of their hands, that they should not worship demons and idols . . . ."[12] It actually seems more cruel to force a person to go through numerous life cycles than to give him ample opportunity in one lifetime to establish a saving relationship with God.

The Bible clearly teaches that there is a day appointed for judgment of all men, living and dead. It also teaches that God the Father will not be our judge, but Jesus, God the Son. John 5:22-23 tells us: "For neither doth the Father judge any man, but he hath given all judgment unto the Son, that all may honor the Son even as they honor the Father. He that honoreth not the Son honoreth not the Father who sent him."

If Jesus, then, is to be our judge, it is imperative that we be on good terms with Him. "Kiss the son," we are told in the

Second Psalm, "lest he be angry, and ye perish in the way, For his wrath will soon be kindled. Blessed are they that take refuge in him."

Judgment is inevitable. But an escape has been provided. Romans 8:1 says: "There is therefore now no condemnation to them that are in Christ Jesus." There really is going to be a day of accounting, and it just makes sense to have the judge on your side.

Walter Martin, a missionary to the cults, tells the following, perhaps brutal, story of three men in hell:

"Boy," said the Protestant, "I wish I had done what the preacher told me to and I wouldn't be here."

"Me, too," said the Catholic. "If I had done what the priest said I wouldn't be here."

The Christian Scientist said, "I'm not here. I'm not here."

Because of sin the judgment of death has

come upon mankind. Denial of this is more than unrealistic.

It is a doctrine of demons.

Chapter 4

"No, Jonathan, there is no such place. Heaven is not a place, and it is not a time. Heaven is being perfect."

Chiang to Jonathan
Part II

Since the time Cain killed his brother, human history has been one long, seemingly endless procession of immorality, hatred, murder, greed, sorcery, drunkenness, war and evil desire. Violence has consistently been the order of the day.

The testimony of Scripture is always the same: man, since the entrance of sin into the world, is lost, unable to help himself, alienated from God, and consequently from his fellow man. Listen to the description of human nature found in Romans 3:10-18:

There is none righteous, no, not one;
There is none that understandeth,
There is none that seeketh after God;
They have all turned aside, they are
    together become unprofitable;
There is none that doeth good, no, not
    so much as one:
Their throat is an open sepulchre;
With their tongues they have used
    deceit:
The poison of asps is under their lips:
Whose mouth is full of cursing and
    bitterness:
Their feet are swift to shed blood;
Destruction and misery are in their ways;
And the ways of peace they have not
    known:
There is no fear of God before their
    eyes."

The Bible further teaches that God took
pity on man's inability to overcome his own
corrupt nature and intervened in human

history in a unique way to deliver him not only from the effects of his nature, but from that nature itself. II Corinthians tells us that "God was in Christ reconciling the world unto himself."[1]

This intervention made possible peace between man and God through Jesus, and the penalty of the sin that separated men from their Creator was taken away. Colossians 2:11 says: " . . . God has now made (you) to share in the very life of Christ! He has forgiven you all your sins: Christ has utterly wiped out the damning evidence of broken laws and commandments which always hung over our heads, and has completely annulled it by nailing it over his own head on the cross." (Phillips.)

That is the end of the matter as far as God is concerned. Jesus took man's place in death. He took man's sins on Himself and died once for all—a perfect, sinless sacrifice.

He settled the matter of sin forever on the Cross. That Cross spelled the absolute destruction of the power of Satan. And to put His stamp of approval on the entire transaction, God the Father raised Jesus from the dead.

The denial of the Atonement and Resurrection is the Third Doctrine of Demons.

There are two basic forms this denial takes in our society. The first is a denial of the need for the Atonement; it is the dogged, if euphoria, belief in the perfectability of man. This approach embodies a faulty appreciation of the true nature of man. The idea here is that man is good and learns to be evil, so that when his socially disabling environment is replaced and he is reeducated, man will be more or less perfect in and of himself.

Erich Fromm, one of America's most influential psychiatrists, has written a book called *You Shall Be As Gods* in which he states that what happened in the Garden of Eden was not the "fall" of man, but the beginning of his rise, by breaking the "incestuous ties with blood and soil." In other words, until man broke with God, he was not free to be himself—to maximize himself.

It would seem, however, that man has not risen very far. The average man today is no better than Cain. The average city is hardly an improvement over Sodom and Gommorah. And the average metropolitan newspaper is only an echo of millenia of historical records. It is time to face one inescapable fact: there has never been any moral evolution.

Men are resistent to change; so resistent, in fact, that unless God does a sovereign work in their hearts, they are lost. This is what the Atonement is all about. It is really very simple.

A deaconess in a major denomination once made the comment that she had a hard time taking Communion because she was convinced that the Crucifixion was all a terrible mistake. She obviously had no understanding of the simplicity of the Atonement. It is this: Because of sin, man was under the sentence of eternal death, but God sent His only begotten Son to do man's dying for him. Now, by accepting this substitution, man is restored to fellowship with God the Father and receives a new nature. II Corinthians 5:17 tells us: "If any man is in Christ he is a new creature." That is, one who accepts Jesus as his Savior becomes a new and different person.

The old man cannot be perfected. That is the devil's lie, and as long as Satan can keep people trying to pull themselves and others up by their bootstraps, he can keep them from the Cross where the real work has already been done.

You cannot perfect the old man . . . but he can be made into a new man. He can have a new birth. Jesus told Nicodemus that unless a man were born again, he could not see the Kingdom of Heaven.[2] Paul instructed the church members at Colossae in righteous living, "Seeing you have put off the old man with his doings, and have put on the new man, that is being renewed unto knowledge after the image of him that created him . . . ."[3]

And where does this new man come from; what is his origin? He is a creation of God the Father, and is a result of faith in the person and work of Jesus Christ. John puts it this way: "But to as many as received him (Jesus), gave he the right to become the children of God, even to them that believe on his name, who were born, not of blood, nor of the will of the flesh, nor of the will of man, but of God."[4] It is up to God to do His sovereign work.

The other denial of the Atonement generally takes this form: "To be saved you have to accept Jesus and . . . ." Walter Martin says that "Jesus and . . ." is the basic tenet of all the cults. It is a refusal to accept the *adequacy* of the work done on the Cross.

This is merely man's refusing to admit there is nothing he can do to help God out—man's refusing to believe it is really as simple as just believing. "Surely," man thinks, "there must be *something* one needs to do besides having faith. It hardly seems like enough, really!"

Most people think that good works are what is really necessary to get one into good standing with God, and that if one stays within the limits of socially acceptable behavior, gives money to charity, becomes involved in "worthwhile" causes, avoids murder and extortion, and possibly goes to church in a more or less regular manner, somehow everything will work out all right. Unfortunately for them, God takes a rather dim view of all this.

With respect to good works, it was Martin Luther who laid hold of the key doctrine, a doctrine which triggered what has come to be called the Reformation. That doctrine is found in Romans 1:17 and Galatians 3:11: "the righteous shall live by faith." Not "faith and . . .," not "faith, but . . .," just faith! Paul explains this further: " . . . that life which I now live in the flesh I live in faith, the faith which is in the Son of God who loved me and gave himself up for me."[5]

Verne D. Roberts of the Bolivian Indian Mission tells about questioning a spirit that spoke through a medium during a seance. He asked if the spirit believed in salvation by faith and faith alone. "Yes," it said, "we believe that salvation is by faith and works."

61

Roberts goes on to add that nothing he could say would move the spirit from this declaration.[6]

You see, it's a doctrine that demons insist upon. Yet with His last breath, Christ declared: "It is finished." To believe that there is more to be done is to deny the effect of the Atonement.

God expects good works from His people, most assuredly. But they are to be the issue of faith. Jesus dealt straightforwardly with this matter when the people asked Him: "What must we do that we may work the works of God? Jesus answered and said unto them, This is the work of God, *That ye believe on him whom he hath sent.*"[7]

When Christ confronted Paul on the road to Damascus He delivered to that Jew's Jew this commission as a missionary to the Gentiles: " . . . to open their eyes that they may turn from darkness to light and from the power of Satan unto God, that they may receive the remission of sins and inheritance among them *that are sanctified by faith in me.*"[8]

Any teaching which tries to add something to the Atonement is a denial of the Atonement.

The Resurrection is the proof that the sacrifice on the Cross was sufficient. If Jesus had not been raised, we would never have known for sure that His work had been accepted. Now every believer has the assurance of the same triumph over death. Paul says:

"Now, if the raising of Christ from the dead is the very heart of our message, how can some of you deny there is any resurrection? For if there is no such thing as the resurrection of the dead, then Christ was never raised. And if Christ was not raised, then neither our preaching nor your faith has any meaning at all ... Truly, if our hope in Christ were limited to this life only we should of all mankind, be the most to be pitied.

"But the glorious fact is that Christ *did* rise from the dead: he has become the very first to rise of all who sleep the sleep of death."[9]

The Resurrection isn't just important to the Christian faith; it is vital. The Resurrection disarmed the biggest weapon in Satan's arsenal: death. Small wonder he wants to keep people from finding out about it. And he has assigned some of his most subtle assistants to seeing that the news doesn't leak out.

Chapter 5

"Poor Fletch. Don't believe what your eyes are telling you. All they show is limitation. Look with your understanding, find out what you already know, and you'll see the way to fly."

JLS to Fletcher
Part III

The laws of logic still taught in all beginning math courses state that you cannot reason from falsehood to truth. That is, if you begin with a principle which is untrue, you can never arrive at the truth from that point. That is why it is so important to understand the basic teachings or doctrines. They lay the foundation for further teaching, and once you accept the basic principle, you are more or less obliged to accept the conclusions that follow.

The doctrines of demons have a purpose that never varies. They are designed to lead men into error and lure them from God. When these doctrines are accepted, they invariably accomplish their end.

We live in a yearning world. All the earth cries out for peace and plenty, for relief. But instead of relief there is confusion, and instead of peace there is violence. Men everywhere are experiencing the need of something bigger than themselves to take control and bring order from this chaos.

All the world's religions are man's attempt to make contact with god or gods and somehow appease them. All these religions, then, are based on human endeavor. This is true from the animist who leaves food offerings in front of a tree to the humanist who commits his life to efforts to bring about peace and prosperity. It is sometimes difficult to see the connection between these two, but it is there. Both of them are trying to secure the same thing—an end to evil.

But the evil persists because the source of evil has not been cut off. Actually, the animist is much closer to the truth than is the humanist. The animist, at least, recognizes the personality of evil. It is very frustrating to modern man to work so hard for good with so little success. But he has never known (or never believed) what the Bible teaches about what man is really up against and what he can do about it.

"Put on God's complete armor," we are advised in Ephesians 6:11-12, "so that you can successfully resist all of the devil's methods of attack. For our fight is not against any physical enemy: it is against organizations and powers that are spiritual. We are up against the unseen power that controls this dark world, and spiritual agents from the very headquarters of evil." (Phillips.)

71

These doctrines of demons come from "the very headquarters of evil," and their purpose is to destroy. Satan's purpose is always to destroy, and he has been perfecting his tools for centuries. If you accept, even by a nod, these basic teachings, the result is just as the devil has planned.

First this: disbelief in the person and work of Jesus Christ means that God is not credible. If you cannot believe everything He says, then you cannot believe anything He says.

Many people accept demonic doctrines and never realize it because the teachings are so subtly disguised. But Christians, whether they realize it or not, are locked in deadly combat with a spiritual enemy, and they need to examine their beliefs. What do you really believe?

Do you believe that Jesus was born of a virgin? If not, how can you believe that Jesus was unique, God in flesh? Can you disbelieve the Virgin Birth and believe in the Incarnation?

Do you believe that all men are basically good, and that evil is due to environment? If so, then what do you think about sin and judgment? Don't take Jonathan's advice. Instead, take a good, hard look at the world and man's limitations before you answer this. To deny sin is to deny the Savior.

Do you believe that all religions are equally good, and all men are going toward God in their separate ways? If all these ways were equally good, then why would God the Father give His only Son to die? Doesn't it stand to reason that He would have chosen some less painful way to make peace—*if* He could have. If you think there is some other, equally good way to God, you are denying the Atonement.

Do you believe the first eight chapters of

Genesis? Not sure? Then can you believe John 3:16? It is time to face these issues squarely.

Paul was greatly concerned that the Gentile churches should have a grasp on the truths of the Christian faith and not be led into error. Romans 16:17-18 says: "Now I beseech you, brethren, mark them that are causing the divisions and occasions of stumbling, contrary to the doctrine which ye learned: and turn away from them. For they are such that serve not our Lord Christ, but their own belly; and by their smooth and fair speech they beguile the hearts of the innocent."

He is sterner with the Galatians: "I marvel that ye are so quickly removing from him who called you in the grace of Christ unto a different gospel; which is not another gospel only there be some that trouble you and would pervert the gospel of Christ. But though we or an angel from heaven should preach to you any gospel other than that which we preached unto you, let him be anathema [accursed of God]. As we have said before, so say I now again, if any man preacheth unto you any gospel other than that which ye received, let him be anathema."[1]

The logical end of the teachings of demons is in sight. There is a cumulative effect in demonic rationale. It is not usually thought out all at once in so orderly a manner, but it goes this way: "If man is really good, and Jesus was not God incarnate, but only a good teacher and example, then he died martyred by the religious system, and not as man's substitute. Now, all this is just the opposite of what the Bible teaches; so the Bible must not be true. If there is a God, He has left man on his own. Therefore, it is up to man to straighten out world affairs by his own intellect.

"But things are not really getting any better. In fact, they may really be getting worse. There may be lulls, but there is never any end to fighting. Now there are getting to be more people than can be fed. The earth's very atmosphere has become contaminated. We have weapons that can blot humanity off the face of the globe. Injustice abounds. There is not enough time left to solve the pollution and population problems before we pollute and populate ourselves out of existence. There is no way for man to get better. And the best minds in the world all working together are unable to solve all these problems before it is too late . . . too late."

This is the point to which man must come when he is on his own. He must finally see that there is no hope. The logical conclusion of the doctrines of demons is this: *Despair is the ultimate reality.*

Have you ever wondered why people do the things they do to escape from reality?

76

Why do they drink? Why do they take drugs? Why do they work so hard or play so hard? It is because reality is unendurable when there is no hope. The people who are fleeing down these roads, which they hope will lead to escape, are living suicides. They are trying to kill, or at least to numb, that part of them that hurts, the part that holds both fear and guilt . . . and somehow they never get away. Consequently many of them become dead suicides.

A large segment of the hospital beds in the United States are in mental wards, and these beds are always full. There is one single cause of this, and that is guilt. No matter what form it takes, all neuroses are basically unresolved guilt. Get rid of guilt and the hospitals could be emptied.

There is nothing man can do to rid himself of his burden of guilt. The millions of dollars spent on psychiatric care each year testify to that. The suicide rate, alcoholism and drug statistics tell the story of despair, and the future doesn't look any better than the past.

"Look with your understanding..." Jonathan Seagull tells Fletcher. And what will you see?—a world in which a golden age of peace, justice, and prosperity is just dawning? "... find out what you already know, and you'll see the way to fly." And what do you already know?—that man is the answer? Look again.

> "Trust in the Lord with all thine heart;
> and lean not unto thine own
> understanding.
>
> In all thy ways acknowledge him,
> and he shall direct thy paths."

says Proverbs 3:5-6 (KJV). God has a better idea.

God can handle the problem of guilt and despair. In fact, He handled it 2000 years ago on a cross outside the walls of Jerusalem. He took man's sin and guilt on Himself, and every man who accepts that substitution becomes free of his guilty burden. He is forgiven.[2]

There is just nothing like forgiveness for getting rid of guilt. But you don't really accept God's forgiveness if you keep trying to make it on your own. You are not really believing Him if you are partially believing the teachings of the world. The Bible makes this very clear: "Ye cannot drink the cup of the Lord, and the cup of demons: ye cannot partake of the table of the Lord and of the table of demons."[3] In other words, you can't have it both ways.

It is necessary to know what the devil is up to in order not to be seduced by his doings. There is a desolation predicted upon the works of Satan and upon those whom he uses:

"And he (the angel) cried with a mighty

voice saying, Fallen, fallen is Babylon the Great, and is become a habitation of demons, and a hold of every unclean spirit and a hold of every unclean and hateful bird." (Revelation 18:2.)

Never forget one thing—seagulls are scavengers.

Notes

Unless otherwise stated, all Scripture quotations are from the American Standard Bible, 1901 edition.

CHAPTER 1

1. John 8:44.
2. Philippians 1:9-10.
3. I Peter 5:8
4. II Corinthians 11:14-15.

CHAPTER 2

1. *Time*, November 13, 1972.
2. John 3:16.
3. Merrill Unger, *The Haunting of*

> *Bishop Pike* (Wheaton, Illinois:
> Tyndale House Publishers, 1968),
> p. 42.

4. *Demon Experience in Many Lands*
   (Chicago, Illinois: Moody Press,
   1960), p. 40.
5. John 14:6.

CHAPTER 3

1. Isaiah 64:6, KJV.
2. Joseph Wolpe, *The Practice of
   Behavior Therapy* (New York:
   Pergamon Press, 1969), p. 20.
3. I John 1:18.
4. Romans 6:23.
5. Matthew 25:41.
6. Matthew 11:14.
7. Job 16:22.
8. Proverbs 11:7.
9. Ezekiel 18:4.

10. Luke 16:22.
11. Revelation 20:12-15.

CHAPTER 4

1. II Corinthians 5:19.
2. John 3:1-6.
3. Colossians 3:8-10.
4. John 1:12-13.
5. Galatians 2:20.
6. *Demon Experience in Many Lands* p. 69.
7. John 6:28-29.
8. Acts 26:18.
9. I Corinthians 15:12-14, 19-20.

CHAPTER 5

1. Galatians 1:6-9.
2. I John 1:9.
3. I Corinthians 10:21.